The Healing Letter

How Writing Can Help You Process and
Overcome Difficult Experiences

The Healing Letter

How Writing Can Help You Process and
Overcome Difficult Experiences

C. HENNIS

Library of Congress Cataloging-in-Publication Data
Author: C. Hennis, M.S.
Title: *The Healing Letter: How Writing Can Help You Process and Overcome Difficult Emotions*
Subjects: Self-Help, Letter Writing, Psychology
ISBN:
Paperback: 979-8-218-95412-3
Hardcover: 979-8-218-95681-3

Cover image by: C. Hennis, M.S.
Book design by: C. Hennis, M.S.

First print edition, 2023, in the United States.

10 9 8 7 6 5 4 3 2 1

To all those who believed in me.
To my heavenly father. The rock I stand on.
To my parents. I love you.
To my beautiful daughters. You are indeed the light of my life.
To my late husband, Jeremy. Who is love and support? I deeply miss you.
To the therapist behind the therapist, I am here to guide you through this journey. As a licensed therapist, I have witnessed the transformative power of therapeutic letter writing in my practice and personal life.
And to all those who are on a journey to healing and wellness. I applaud your courage.

Contents

INTRODUCTION

Have you ever struggled to express your emotions or to make sense of difficult experiences? Have you ever wished you could find a way to heal from past hurts or cultivate greater self-compassion and gratitude?

Therapeutic letter writing may be the answer you are looking for. Writing a letter can provide a safe, structured way to process your emotions and experiences and connect with yourself and others meaningfully. You might be working through a complex relationship, grieving the loss of a loved one, or simply looking to deepen your self-awareness; therapeutic letter writing can help.

Therapeutic letter writing is a transformative tool for emotional healing, self-reflection, and personal growth. It provides a safe space to express thoughts and feelings that may be difficult to verbalize, allowing individuals to process grief, trauma, or unresolved emotions. Whether the letter is to a lost loved one, an estranged friend, or even to oneself, putting words to emotions can provide relief, insight, and, at times, a sense of closure.

In this book, you will learn how to write various therapeutic letters, each with its unique purpose and benefits. You will discover how to structure your letter, what to include, and how to process your emotions while writing. You will also read examples of effective therapeutic letters and learn how they have helped others in their healing journey.

Therapeutic letter writing combines the benefits of journaling and expressive writing with the structure of personal dialogue. Research has shown that writing about one's emotions can reduce stress, improve mental well-being, and promote healing after loss or trauma. It helps to externalize the pain, making it feel more manageable and can provide a tangible way to track emotional progress over time.

This book is for anyone seeking personal growth, healing, or greater self-awareness. Whether you are collaborating with a therapist or simply looking for a way to connect with yourself and others, therapeutic letter writing can be a powerful tool for transformation. So, grab a pen, and let us get started on this journey together.

The Road Map

This book is structured to guide you through therapeutic letter writing, one step at a time. The chapters focus on letters to lost loved ones, letters of closure, forgiveness letters, letters to your younger or future self, and more. You will find:

- **A deep dive into each type of letter**—why it matters, how it can help, and when to use it.
- **Guidance on how to write your letters**, including prompts to help you get started.
- **Examples of letters** inspiring and a sense of connection.

There is no right or wrong way to use this book. It is designed to empower you to begin your healing process. You can move through it chapter by chapter, writing as you go, or skip the letters that resonate most with you now. You may choose to keep some letters, others you might destroy, and some may remain unfinished. The goal is not perfection but expression—to voice the emotions that need release.

Holding this book means searching for something—understanding, closure, healing, or simply a way to make sense of your feelings. I hope that you will find what you need on these pages. Writing has been my lifeline, and I believe it can be one for you, too.

There is much research behind writing as a tool in the therapy journey. However, please know that this is one tool of many and should not replace a psychotherapist. As a therapist, I understand the importance of professional guidance in healing. I encourage you to use this book in correlation with therapy; if that is not something you can do right now, that is okay, too. Most importantly, you feel supported and understood in your healing journey.

You can skip through the book and pull out the necessary information. You could also collaborate with your therapist, jumping to the letter and working through it together in therapy.

This could also be a book your therapist assigns you as homework. You can move through this book as fast or as slowly as needed. The point is to write your thoughts, feelings, trauma experiences, goals, visions, and dreams.

Writing has always been a part of my life, but I never understood its true power until I lost my husband. In the early days of grief, I felt lost, unable to process the depth of my emotions. My therapist suggested something that, at the time, seemed both simple and impossible—writing letters to him. She encouraged me to pour my feelings onto paper, to say the things I never had the chance to speak, to ask questions that would forever remain unanswered, and to express the love that still lived inside me.

At first, I resisted. How could writing to someone who would never read my words help? But as I picked up my pen and let the emotions spill onto the page, I found an unexpected sense of relief. Writing became my way of holding onto him while learning to let go. It allowed me to process my grief, acknowledge my pain, and eventually find a path forward.

This book was born from that profound personal experience, but its purpose extends beyond grief. Therapeutic letter writing is a powerful tool for anyone navigating emotions that feel too big, too complicated, or overwhelming to speak aloud. Whether you are struggling with loss, unresolved conflict, forgiveness, gratitude, or self-reflection, writing can offer a space for healing.

Chapter One

How Writing Heals and Where to Start

" *Writing is medicine. It is an appropriate antidote to injury. It is an appropriate companion for any difficult change.*" – **Julia Cameron.**

There are moments when emotions can feel burdensome, too heavy to carry, too tangled to sort through. Grief, anger, regret, and even love can sit within us, unspoken, weighing us down. In these moments, words written in any form typed on the screen, pen to paper, or even scribbled on a napkin can untangle us. Writing is more than just an act of expression; it is a tool for healing, a way to process the emotions we may not have the space or courage to speak aloud.

I discovered the power of therapeutic letter writing after the death of my spouse. In the depths of my despair, my therapist gave me a simple but daunting assignment: write him a letter. At first, I resisted. It sounded stupid. What is the point? He would never be here to read it. The words would only echo in the space where he used to be—his *Chair*. But eventually, I picked up my pen and let the words spill out. I told him how much I missed him, how angry I was that he was not here, and how lost I felt in the life we were supposed to share. We would have finally made it. And at that moment, something surprising happened. As I wrote, the weight on my shoulders shifted just slightly. The words did not bring him back, but they gave my hurt and pain a place to go. So, I kept writing.

This is why I authored this book. Whether you are grieving a loss like I am struggling with forgiveness or even searching for self-understanding, writing can help you understand what feels impossible to untangle. Through letters, we can say what we never got to say, release emotions that feel too big to hold, and find clarity amid uncertainty. This chapter will explore why writing is such a powerful tool for healing and how it can be the first step toward processing pain, finding closure, and moving forward.

Benefits Of Letter Writing

Therapeutic letter writing has several benefits, including: Emotional processing: Writing about your thoughts and emotions can help you process and make sense of difficult experiences. It can also help you release pent-up emotions safely and healthily. Self-reflection: Writing about your experiences can help you better understand yourself, your values, and your beliefs. It can also help you identify patterns in your behavior and relationships.

- Relationship building: Writing letters to others, whether they are sent or not, can help you express emotions and communicate more effectively. It can also help you strengthen your relationships by providing a safe space for open and honest communication. (Smyth, 1998)
- Increased self-awareness: Writing about your experiences can help you better understand your emotions, behaviors, and reactions. This increased self-awareness can lead to personal growth and improved decision-making. (Pennebaker J. W., 1997)
- Stress relief: Writing can be a therapeutic and calming activity that helps reduce stress and anxiety. It can provide a sense of release and relief from overwhelming emotions. (Pennebaker J. W., 1997)
- Improved physical health: Research has shown that therapeutic writing can positively affect physical health, including improving immune system functioning and reducing symptoms of chronic illness. (Baikie, 2005)

Therapeutic letter writing can be powerful for emotional healing, personal growth, and relationship building.

Misconceptions About Letter Writing

A few common misconceptions about therapeutic letter writing may prevent some people from trying it or limit its perceived usefulness. Here are a few of these misconceptions and why they are not necessarily true:

- *Only for people with specific diagnoses or backgrounds.* Some people may assume that therapeutic letter writing is only helpful for people with particular diagnoses or backgrounds, such as those who have experienced trauma or struggle with mental health issues. However, therapeutic letter writing can benefit anyone who wants to process their emotions, gain insight into themselves, or improve their relationships.
- *Requires writing skill or creativity.* Some people may feel intimidated by writing a therapeutic letter if it requires a certain level of writing skill or imagination. However, therapeutic letter writing is not about producing a polished piece but expressing yourself honestly and authentically in whatever feels most comfortable.
- *Requires a specific format or structure.* Some may assume therapeutic letter writing requires a particular format or structure, such as beginning with an exact phrase or ending with a specific reflection. However, there is no "right" way to write a therapeutic letter; it can take many forms, depending on your goals and preferences.
- *Only valid for specific types of problems.* Some people may assume that therapeutic letter writing is only helpful for particular problems, such as relationship issues or grief. However, therapeutic letter writing can be applied to various situations and concerns, from work stress to existential questions.

Therapeutic letter writing can benefit emotional processing, self-reflection, and relationship building. We can better understand ourselves and others by putting our thoughts and feelings into words. We may experience improvements in our mental and physical health.

Steps in the Therapeutic Letter Writing Process

1. **Determine the recipient:** Consider who the letter is for. Is it for a loved one or for another individual in your world that caused hurt and pain?
2. **Consider an outline first:** Writing the letter's overall structure first helps gauge a few things. It aids in beginning to see the letter take form. It can show areas that will be emotionally charged or more challenging to write.
3. **Write the letter:** Begin by acknowledging your experiences and feelings. Use the feelings wheel to place down precisely what emotions are coming forward. Write about situations that occurred, outcomes, and how those things/events made you feel, how it affected your abilities or being today. Do not worry about form, structure, or spelling. If it is helpful, consider writing the letter in chunks or sections. Use notecards or an outline.

Note: Remember, a feelings wheel can be found here: https://feelingswheel.com/

4. **Review and edit**: Once the letter is written, review it for clarity. Do you have everything you want to say or would say to this individual if they were standing before you? Ensure that the language is appropriate and conveys your true feelings. Consider whether it achieves the intended purpose you are trying to make.
5. **Decide whether to share the letter**: Discuss it with a friend, therapist, or family member and gain their perspective. Use the letter to continue the therapeutic process and support the healing journey. The letter was written with the idea that you are freeing yourself from your emotional captivity. You and only you can decide whether or not to share the letter with the individual it regards. There are several options: if you do not want to

share it, you can burn it, release the pages, or hide it in a journal or other private keepsake.

☆ **Note:** Make sure the way you release the letter does not harm yourself, someone else, or the planet.

Consider that this is your journey. Remember that therapeutic letters should be tailored to each person's needs and relationships. I remember the first time I sat down to write to my husband after he passed. My therapist had encouraged me to write to him, but I had no idea where to begin. I felt silly, angry, and heartbroken all at once. Eventually, I picked up my pen and let the words come, unfiltered and raw. Here is an excerpt from one of those early letters:

March 23rd, 2022
My Dearest Jeremy, Another few days have passed since I ran my fingers through your hair. I am worried I will forget what your hands feel like in mine. How much I miss you. I walk around, hoping to see any piece of you I can. Like in the birds that fly, in the sun setting, or any piece of you I could capture. Life today seems so unbearable without you. There are days I cannot even function, let alone excel, because you are not with me. I miss being able to send you a quick text message or phone call to hear your voice. So, it is back to the old-fashioned handwritten letters next to your chair, hoping you will come home and read them. So, how do I do this? This living each day without you? I feel like this is a prison sentence. I have fifty years to live without you. I am stuck here on earth where I am not living; I am just going through the motions. Days when I cannot even do my job, and more days continue to slip past me. Nothing seems to take away this pain. The kids often withstand the worst of the pain I feel. My overarching pain. I promise you that I will work harder to make it work. I have made a ton of mistakes when it comes to our children. I would give anything to hear your voice or have five minutes with you again. I Love You. C

After writing this, I did not feel healed; grief does not work like that. But I did feel different. The emotions that had been spinning inside me, overwhelming and directionless, finally had a place to land.

One of the most healing aspects of letter writing is that it permits us to express emotions we often suppress. We live in a world that expects grief to be neat and to have a precise end date. But loss does not work like that. Writing allowed me to say things I did not feel comfortable speaking aloud—to express my anger, sadness, love, and longing without fear of judgment. Here is one of the letters I wrote on a day when the grief did not feel so heavy—when I was beginning to realize that healing does not mean forgetting:

June 27th, 2022
Hey, Sweetheart; I hope this note finds its way to your mailbox in heaven. Sorry it has been a while since I wrote; many things have happened. I have missed you. I have kept all my promises to you. The deck looks great. I have put lights on it as you like. My family has been up. We were able to catch up on all the maintenance that needed to be done around the house. The property is looking good. I am still working in your garden. Not entirely done yet. The girls are missing you. And the new puppy is a handful. I quit my job to be with the kids over the summer and to study for the licensure exam. The dryer broke again. So, I am hoping that is not going to be another expense. I am overwhelmed. I am trying to breathe; it is just really hard. I hope you are doing okay. I Love You. C

This is why letter writing has such power. It allows us to express our grief, forgiveness, or whatever we want to process and process in real-time. It gives us space to document our emotions as they move and change. Looking back on our words, we notice we are still moving forward, even in the most challenging moments.

Things To Consider

There are several things I would like you to consider when beginning this process:

- **Set an intention**: Before writing, ask some questions. What do you hope to gain from the process? Is there a specific issue you want to address or an emotion you want to process? Having a clear intention can guide your writing and focus your thoughts.

- **Choose a private and safe space:** Find a confidential and safe space where you can write without distractions or interruptions. This can help you feel more comfortable and secure when exploring difficult emotions or memories.

- **Consider the timing**: Consider the best time to write. Some people find it helpful to write in the morning, while others prefer to write at night. Choose a time that works best for you, and stick to a regular schedule.

- **Use a pen and paper**: While typing on a computer is an option, using a pen and paper can help you feel more connected to the writing process and can also help you feel less distracted.

- **Be gentle with yourself:** Therapeutic letter writing can bring up strong emotions, and it is essential to be gentle throughout the process. Take breaks when needed and allow yourself to feel whatever feelings come up without judgment.

- **Identify your goals**: Before diving into the book, it is helpful to identify what you hope to gain from therapeutic letter writing. Are you looking to process emotions, reflect on your life, build relationships, set goals, or explore creativity? Knowing your goals can help you focus on the areas that are most relevant to you.

- **Take breaks and reflect:** After each section, take some time to reflect on what you have learned and how you can apply it to your life. Consider taking a break from writing your therapeutic letter. Sometimes, just sitting with the emotions and just observing them also helps.

- **Use the examples:** The book includes practical examples to help readers apply the concepts to their lives. Use these examples to practice writing your therapeutic letters and better understand the process.

- **Start with an outline:** Start writing an outline first, or use notecards to organize your thoughts more easily. This will make the writing process more manageable when you start.

- **Most Importantly! Seek support if needed**: If you struggle with difficult emotions or memories, consider seeking help from a therapist or mental health professional. They can provide guidance and support as you explore your feelings through writing.
- **Stop if you need to**: During this process, there will be times that it becomes overwhelming. That is okay. However, I always tell my clients to stop if it gets too triggering. Please pick it up at another time or seek support (family, friends, therapist) and then keep going. But know that you got this.

It is essential to recognize that therapeutic letter writing is a flexible and adaptable tool that can be used by anyone who wants to explore their emotions, thoughts, and relationships. While it may be beneficial for people experiencing emotional distress or mental health issues, it can also be helpful for those who want to deepen their self-awareness, connect with others, or foster personal growth.

The Physical Benefits of Writing

Writing has long been a form of self-expression and a way to tell stories, document history, and share thoughts. But beyond communication, writing has another remarkable purpose: a tool for healing. Studies have shown that expressive writing helps regulate emotions, reduces anxiety, and improves immune functioning. But why does writing have such a profound effect on the mind and body?

When we experience emotional distress, our thoughts can become overwhelmed, making it hard to process what we are feeling and experiencing. Dr. James Pennebaker, a leading researcher in expressive writing, has found that writing about traumatic experiences for 15-20 minutes daily over several days can improve mental well-being. (Pennebaker, 1997) (Pennebaker J. W., 1986) His research has revealed that people who write about their deepest thoughts and feelings report fewer depressive symptoms, lower stress levels, and fewer doctor trips. Who does not like that?

Writing is so helpful because it provides structure to our thoughts. When we write, we are forced to organize our emotions, which can help us make more sense of the painful things we are experiencing. Instead of carrying these painful emotions in an unprocessed weighted form, we can begin to see them more clearly, which aids us in moving through them.

Moreover, writing can give us control over experiences that might otherwise feel uncontrollable. (Pennebaker J. W., 1997) Grief, trauma, and loss often make us feel downright powerless. But when we write, we can actively confront those demons and shape the narrative. Even when we cannot change what has happened to us, we can change how we choose to carry it.

Surprisingly, writing does not just benefit our mental health; it can also improve our physical health. Studies have shown that engaging in expressive writing is linked to our body lowering blood pressure, a more muscular immune system and functioning, and faster healing from injuries. (Smyth, 1998) How does this all work, you ask? Well, emotional stress can take a toll on the body, and it can lead to chronic inflammation, weakened immune responses, and an increased risk of illness and even heart attack. Writing reduces stress.

The Journal of American Medical Association produced a study regarding chronic illnesses. The studies showed that individuals with chronic diseases who engaged in expressive writing showed an improved immune system response, suggesting that writing helped regulate the body's stress response. (Smyth, 1998) Another study found that individuals who wrote about emotional distress recovered more quickly from surgery than those who didn't. (Koschwanez, 2013) These findings reinforce what many instinctively feel: writing provides a form or release.

Why Letter Writing is Especially Powerful

While journaling and free writing are beneficial, letter writing offers something different. It provides a sense of connection to self. When we write a letter, we are not just expressing ourselves; we are expressing our emotions and directing them toward someone, even if they never read the words. This can make it easier to say what we are thinking and feeling. We can process grief, find closure, release resentment, and gain self-compassion by writing to our past or future selves.

I did not realize how much I needed it when I wrote to my late husband. My words were filled with hurt, anger, sadness, and my love for him. But in writing to him, I felt a renewed sense of connection, even in his absence. It reminded me that our bond was not gone with the loss; it simply changed.

Writing is a tool—not a cure, a quick fix, but a way forward. It gives us space to feel, reflect, and begin making sense of the things we may never fully understand. I will guide you through several therapeutic letters for grief, forgiveness, self-discovery, and release in the following chapters. You will find examples and prompts to write your letters. I hope this book will be something you read and use—a place for your words, emotions, and healing.

Chapter Two

Letters as Medicine

*" Healing takes courage, and we all have courage, even if we have to dig a little to find it." – **Tori Amos.***

Therapeutic letter writing is a deeply personal endeavor that can take many forms depending on the emotions and situation you are trying to process. Each type of letter serves a unique purpose: closure, self-reflection, emotional processing, or goal setting.

For example, a closure letter is written when someone needs to release lingering emotions about a person or a situation. This often brings a sense of resolution to the individual. These letters can be written to loved ones who have passed away, former partners, estranged family members, therapists, or even a former version of yourself. Additionally, a letter to the deceased is about closure and a connection with someone not here.

Other therapeutic letters provide a way to communicate with oneself from a place of kindness and understanding. These letters can be written as encouragement during self-doubt or regret. Similarly, letters to a future or past self. This allows the writer to recognize personal growth, offer wisdom to their younger self, or set intentions for the future. The different letters provided the comfort needed for the selected letter.

Therapeutic letters are used in various forms of psychotherapy to facilitate the therapeutic process. These letters can take many forms, depending on the specific therapeutic approach and the goals within therapy. Therapeutic letters are also written in a personal form aside from treatment. Some individuals are intimidated by the therapy process for whatever reason, and that is fine. Therapeutic letters can also be a self-guided journey through your situations or pain to find healing. Here are some of the several types of therapeutic letters:

Goodbye/Closure Letters: Closure Letters, as they have become known, help resolve unresolved relationships or situations. These can be relationships with your therapist, ex-boyfriend, or girlfriend, anything about the past, or making peace with a problem or circumstance that has ended the relationship. It aids in releasing lingering pain, regret, or unanswered questions about someone no longer in your life. Therapeutic goodbye letters can be used when a therapeutic relationship ends. These letters allow clients to express their thoughts and feelings about the therapy process and meaningfully say goodbye to the therapist. More types of these letters would include a letter to a severed relationship, letters to a deceased loved one, and ending unhealthy relationships. Goodbye letters are another form of this. This could be saying goodbye to someone who died (husband, friend, child, unborn baby), a relationship ending for whatever reason, or any other goodbye circumstance.

Narrative letters: Narrative letters are a form of therapy in which you are encouraged to write about your experiences, thoughts, and feelings. These letters are usually addressed to a particular individual. They can help you reflect on your experiences and gain insight into your feelings.

Creative and Expressive letters: Expressive letters are written to express intense emotions that you may find difficult to communicate in person. These letters can be addressed to anyone you wish, including someone who caused pain or discomfort. These letters blend therapeutic writing with imagination and artistry. Whether through poetry, storytelling, or metaphor, they offer an open-ended way to explore emotions and self-expression.

Unsent letters: Unsent letters are written to communicate thoughts and feelings that you may not want to express directly to another person. These letters can be used to process anger, sadness, or disappointment.

Gratitude letters: Gratitude letters express appreciation and thanks to someone who has positively impacted the person's life. These letters can help you to focus on positive experiences and to feel more connected to the people in your life.

Self-compassion/ Self-Reflection Letters: These letters are written to practice self-compassion and self-care. These letters are addressed to the self and can help you to develop a more positive and compassionate view of yourself. These could include letters to your future self, letters to your past self, and letters to your present self. Writing to yourself with kindness and understanding can help reduce self-hatred and combat self-criticism. These letters encourage self-forgiveness, encouragement, and acknowledgment of personal growth, fostering a more compassionate inner dialogue.

Forgiveness letters: A therapeutic letter is used to help someone process and work through feelings of anger, resentment, or hurt towards another person. It involves writing a letter to the person who has wronged you, expressing your feelings and thoughts about the situation and its impact on you. The letter aims to help you work through your emotions and move toward forgiveness and healing.

Trauma Letters: A trauma letter is used to help process locked emotions regarding several types of traumas. These letters are typically written to an individual who committed abuse to you or someone you loved. These letters can also be about processing a traumatic event, such as seeing war, terrorism, or some other horror.

Younger Self Letters: Younger Self Letters offer wisdom, reassurance, and validation for the love that has shaped the person that you are now. These letters help process the past trials, heal old wounds, and recognize the resilience you have built over time.

Future Self Letters: A future letter is a type of letter that can be written to your future self. These letters can include goals or things you want to accomplish or just yourself. These letters serve as a message of hope and accountability for the person you are to become. They often include a reflection on the current challenges that you are facing, aspirations, and reminders of what truly matters in life. This provides a perspective and motivation when revisiting later.

Spiritual Letters: A letter conveys feelings to a higher being or deity you believe in. These letters are there to process any prayer requests or situations you need further guidance on.

Emotional Processing Letters (Letters to Pain, Fear, or Grief): Emotional Processing Letters explore and untangle the overwhelming emotions that often arise in response to a significant event. Unlike expressive letters, which focus on free-flowing emotions, emotional processing letters help make sense of tangled feelings. These letters also let you personify difficult emotions, allowing you to externalize and confront them more deeply.

Relationship Building Letters: Relationship Building Letters are intended to strengthen the connections within the relationship you are building presently. These letters process appreciation, love, or apology. They can end broken relationships and deepen or share gratitude with those who matter to you.

Goal Setting and Action Planning Letters: Goal Setting Letters are where you begin writing down the goals in a letter. It provides clarity and commitment to yourself. These letters serve as a structured approach to outlining intentions, motivations, and concrete steps to turn aspirations into reality.

It is important to note that therapeutic letters can vary depending on your approach and needs. You can also use a combination of several types of letters to help you achieve your therapeutic goals.

Thoughts on Writing a Therapeutic Letter

Writing a therapeutic letter does not require perfect literary skill or poetic language. What matters is your genuine authenticity and emotional honesty. Some individuals write in a raw, unfiltered style, letting their emotions flow freely onto the page, while others like a more structured approach to their processing style. Organizing thoughts carefully is the hardest part, but try not to overthink them.

A common issue in letter writing is not knowing where or how to start. One effective method is to begin with the simple phrase, "Dear [name or emotion], I have wanted to say this for a long time…" This will help break the initial resistance to writing and encourage the words to flow naturally. Another way to consider is whether or not to send the letter. Some letters are meant to be read by their recipient, while others only serve as a private tool for personal healing and growth. Sending them would cause more harm to you and them. Those types of letters are processed differently. Deciding whether to keep, destroy, or deliver a letter is the part of the process that can be just as meaningful as writing it.

If a writer finds themselves overwhelmed by emotions while writing, they should **STOP**. Consider taking breaks, stepping away, or returning to the letter when ready. Writing should not feel more like an obligation than a tool for processing emotions.

There is no right or wrong way to write a therapeutic letter. The goal is to get your feelings, thoughts, and pain onto paper. The most significant way to do that is to write. It does not have to follow a specific style or format. The spelling does not have to be perfect. I have included some suggestions if you need help.

- **Identify the purpose**: Start by identifying the letter's intent. What are you hoping to achieve with this letter? Are you expressing gratitude, exploring a challenging experience, or saying goodbye to a time of life, an individual that needs to be removed from your life, or just your pain in general? This step is best achieved in an outline.

- **Address the recipient**: Depending on the letter's purpose, you may address it to the therapist, a specific person, or yourself. This is usually at the very beginning.
- **Be honest and authentic**: Therapeutic letters are meant to be a place where you can be genuine and authentic about your thoughts and feelings. Avoid censoring yourself or trying to present a specific image. Do not worry about format or spelling.
- **Use "I" statements:** Use "I" statements to express your thoughts and feelings. For example, instead of saying, "You make me feel angry," say, "I feel angry when..."
- **Reflect on your experience**: Use the letter to reflect on your experiences and gain insight into your thoughts and feelings. Find personal growth areas and what you might have learned through this situation.

Tips For Processing the Emotion

Therapeutic letter writing can bring up some very intense emotions, and it is imperative to plan how to deal with them when they do. Some people have experienced relief and clarity after writing, while others might feel overwhelmed, raw, and vulnerable. Recognizing and accepting these emotional responses is a big part of the healing journey.

One approach is to engage in self-care before and after writing. This might include deep breathing, meditation, calming music (I love light piano Jazz), or stepping outside. Some find it helpful to write in a safe and comfortable space, ensuring they have privacy and emotional security. I enjoy writing on my couch in the living room, with my television playing light jazz or relaxation music.

Deciding what to do with the letter is another crucial step that needs a plan laid out before starting. Some choose to reread and reflect on their words, while others prefer to set the letter aside and revisit it later. If the emotions feel overwhelming, **STOP**; talking with a trusted friend, therapist, or support group might be beneficial. Moreover, some letters, especially those written for closure, may serve a cathartic purpose of being ritualistically destroyed (such as burning, shredding, or burying them) as a symbolic act of releasing emotions.

Note: I do not recommend releasing them via a balloon; that does more harm to the environment than is helpful.

Since emotions evolve, rewriting letters can also be helpful. It can often offer insight into personal growth. Writing can be a valuable tool for processing emotions but can also be challenging and emotional. Here are some more tips for processing emotions during the writing process:
Create a safe and comfortable space: Find a quiet and cozy room to express yourself without interruption or distraction.
Breathe and relax: Take some deep breaths and relax. This can help to reduce stress and anxiety, allowing you to be more present and focused.

Identify your emotions: Take a moment to identify your feelings. Are you feeling sad, angry, or anxious? Acknowledge and validate your feelings. Use the feelings wheel if you find yourself stuck.

Note: Remember, a feelings wheel can be found here: https://feelingswheel.com/

Use descriptive language: Use descriptive language to describe your emotions and experiences. This can clarify your thoughts and feelings and help your therapist understand your experience.

Write freely: Do not worry about grammar or spelling; write freely without judgment or self-censorship.

Take breaks as needed to process and reflect on your emotions. Do not push yourself too hard if you are feeling overwhelmed. Remember, if it begins to become too much, **STOP**. It is not helpful to get yourself so dysregulated that you cannot function daily.

Focus on self-care: After the writing process, focus on self-care. This can include walking, relaxing, or talking with a trusted friend or therapist.

Remember that processing emotions is gradual, and working through difficult emotions may take time. Be patient and compassionate with yourself, and do not hesitate to reach out for support if needed.

What To Possibility Include in a Therapeutic Letter

While no playbook exists for writing these letters, certain elements can help guide the writing process. Some letters may focus on expressing emotions in the present moment, while others may include reflections on past experiences or hopes for the future.

Questions you can ask yourself are:
- What emotions am I experiencing now, and what do I need to express?
- Is there something I wish I had said but never did?
- What do I hope to gain from writing this letter?
- What message do I want to leave with the recipient (whether a person, a past self, or an emotion)?

If writing to another person, acknowledge the positive and negative aspects of the situation you are addressing. For example, in a goodbye letter to a former partner, it might be helpful to include gratitude for shared memories and sadness for how things ended. If writing about an emotion like grief, a person might highlight the pain while recognizing the newly found strength they have developed to carry such a burden.

A closing statement can also be helpful. It can provide a sense of resolution or meaning, even if the letter remains unopened. Some letters may end with a farewell, a promise, or even a statement of declaration. It often depends on the intention behind the letter and the writing. The content of a therapeutic letter can vary depending on the purpose of the letter and the therapeutic approach. This is not an exhaustive list; it is just to get you started.

Here are some additional things that you may also consider including in a therapeutic letter:

- **Expressions of gratitude**: If you write a gratitude letter, express your appreciation for the person's support, care, and kindness.
- **Descriptions of your experiences**: Describe your experiences and how they have impacted you. This can include describing your thoughts, emotions, and behaviors.
- **Reflections on your thoughts and feelings**: Reflect on your thoughts and feelings and explore how they have influenced your experiences.

Note: Remember, a feelings wheel can be found here: https://feelingswheel.com/

- **Exploration of challenges or difficulties**: If you are writing about a harrowing experience, explore the challenges you faced and how you coped with them. Explain what life has been like for you since this happened.
- **Insights or realizations**: Share any insights or realizations that you have gained from your experiences or the therapeutic process.
- **Acknowledgment of progress**: If you are writing a goodbye letter or reflecting on progress, acknowledge your progress and how it has impacted you.
- **Expression of emotions**: Allow yourself to express yourself freely, using "I" statements to describe how you feel. You can include the pain, hurt, and trauma caused by this situation. Explain how you are coping with carrying such a burden.
- **Closing remarks**: End the letter positively, expressing gratitude, hope, or a sense of closure.

Remember that therapeutic letters are not intended to be perfect, polished writing pieces. They are meant to be a tool for self-reflection and expression and a way to deepen your understanding of your experiences and emotions.

Beyond writing itself, some individuals find meaning in including rituals in the process. Reading a letter aloud, placing it in a meaningful location, or setting it free (by burning, burying, or sending it) can aid in the reinforcement and the emotional impact of the letter. Some decide to keep letters in journals as a record of personal growth. Other individuals have chosen to use them as a private form of communication with someone they have lost.

Therapeutic letter writing, though deeply personal, can be an equally powerful tool for emotional healing and growth. Whether used for closure, self-reflection, or emotional release, writing allows individuals to process their emotions and experiences meaningfully and implicitly. By knowing and understanding the several types of letters, learning how to structure them, and practicing self-care, anyone can use letter writing to free themselves from their hurt and pain while allowing healing and personal growth. As you progress in this book, I encourage you to have an open mind and heart, allowing your words to guide you toward more profound understanding and emotional relief.

As we have explored, therapeutic letter writing is a powerful tool for processing emotions, finding closure, and fostering healing. By understanding the several types of letters and how to write them, you are well-equipped to begin your journey of emotional expression. In Chapter 3, we will combine all this by integrating letter writing into your everyday life, revisiting your letters over time, and exploring ways to share your writing when it feels right. This chapter will empower you to continue your healing journey and use therapeutic writing as an ongoing source of support and growth.

Chapter Three

Exploring Therapeutic Letters

" And now these three remain faith, hope, and love. ... But the greatest of these is love." – 1 Corinthians 13:13

In this chapter, I want to go into more detail about the types of letters I commonly use and provide examples of what they might look like. As you continue this journey, the letters you have written will offer valuable insights into your emotional growth, and revisiting them over time can deepen your understanding of how far you have come.

Writing therapeutic letters can be a continuous source of support and help guide you through everyday challenges and more complex emotional experiences.

Emotional Processing Letters

Emotional processing letters are therapeutic letters that help people process and cope with difficult emotions, experiences, and memories. They are often used in the context of trauma therapy or other forms of psychotherapy.

The purpose of emotional processing letters is to help people express their emotions and experiences in a safe and structured way. By writing about their experiences, people can gain greater insight and understanding of their feelings and the impact that their experiences have had on them.

Emotional processing letters typically involve writing about a specific event or experience that has had a significant emotional impact. The writer is encouraged to describe the event in detail, including their thoughts, emotions, and physical sensations. The letter may also include reflections on the event, its meaning, and the writer's coping strategies and support systems.

The letter is often written as being addressed to a trusted friend or therapist. This can help to create a sense of safety and support for the writer, even if they are not sharing the letter with anyone else. After writing the emotional processing letter, the writer may share it with their therapist or keep it for reflection. The therapist can provide support and guidance as the writer processes their emotions and experiences. Overall, emotional processing letters can be a valuable tool for helping people process and cope with difficult emotions and experiences and can be particularly helpful in trauma therapy.

Here is an example of an Emotional Processing Letter:

Dear [Name],

I am writing about a challenging experience weighing heavily on my mind. A few weeks ago, I argued with a close friend, and we said some hurtful things to each other. Since then, I have felt much anger and sadness about what happened. When we were arguing, I felt so frustrated and powerless. I could not believe that someone I cared about could say such hurtful things to me. I felt like I was being attacked, and I did not know how to defend myself. After the argument, I felt so alone and abandoned. I did not know who to turn to for support.

Since then, I have been struggling to make sense of what happened. I replayed the argument to understand why it happened and what I could have done differently. I feel stuck in this anger, sadness, and regret cycle and do not know how to break free. Writing this letter has been helpful for me. It has allowed me to express my feelings without worrying about judgment or criticism. It has also helped me to see more clearly how the argument has affected me and what I need to do to move forward.

Thank you for being here to listen.

Sincerely, [Your Name]

This is just one example of how an emotional processing letter might look. It is a basic form of this type of letter. I always ask clients to take this a bit further. Dive into your feelings here. The letter's content will vary depending on the individual's experiences and emotions. The most important thing is to be honest and authentic in your writing and use the letter as a tool for self-exploration and healing. A good thing to remember is that it is not about the letter's length but about processing the emotion that matters.

Tips For Getting the Most Out of This

Here are some tips for getting the most out of emotional processing letters:

- **Choose a specific event or experience to write about:** Choose an event or occasion that has significantly impacted you. This can be a traumatic event, a complicated relationship, or a challenging life transition.
- **Set aside time and space**: Find a quiet and comfortable space to write without interruption. Set aside enough time to write freely and without feeling rushed.
- **Write freely**: Allow yourself to write without worrying about grammar, spelling, or punctuation. Write whatever comes to mind, and do not censor yourself.
- **Be descriptive**: Use descriptive language to describe the event or experience, including your thoughts, emotions, and physical sensations. Try to create a vivid picture of what happened and how you felt.
- **Focus on your feelings**: Pay attention to your emotions as you write. Please do not shy away from difficult emotions or try to suppress them. Instead, allow yourself to feel and express them entirely in your writing.

Note: Remember, a feelings wheel can be found here: https://feelingswheel.com/

- **Write for yourself**: Write as if you are talking to yourself or a trusted friend. Do not worry about what others may think or how they may react.

Note: No one needs to see these letters unless you decide to share.

- **Reflect on your experience**: After you have written the letter, take some time to reflect on what you have written. Consider what you have learned about yourself, your emotions, and your coping strategies.
- **Share with your therapist**: If you feel comfortable, share your letter with your therapist. They can help you process your emotions and guide you as you work through your experiences.

Writing Prompts for Emotional Processing Letters

- **Exploring the Emotional Event:** What happened in this situation that triggered intense emotions for you? What feelings are you experiencing now, and how would you describe them? Can you identify past experiences that might have influenced your feelings? How has this emotion impacted your daily life, thoughts, and relationships?
- **Understanding the Feelings:** What do these emotions reveal about your needs, desires, or boundaries? Are there any beliefs or narratives about yourself tied to this emotion? How does this emotion affect your sense of self-worth or personal identity? Can you identify any patterns in your emotional responses to similar situations in the past?
- **Processing the Underlying Causes:** Are there unresolved feelings from the past that may be contributing to this current emotion? What would it take for you to heal from this emotion? What do you wish you could say to the person, the event, or the situation that caused this emotional reaction? How do you feel about confronting this emotion—are you ready, or do you need more time?
- **Exploring Potential Shifts or Reframes**: How can you view this situation or emotion differently? What can you

learn from this experience to help you manage similar situations better? What would it be if you could give yourself advice at this moment? Can you find any positive outcomes or growth that has resulted from feeling this way?

- **Finding Peace and Release**: What would it look like for you to let go of this emotion and move forward? How can you forgive yourself or others to release this emotion? Is there a symbol or action (such as breathing, letting go, or visualizing peace) that helps you process and release this emotion?

Self-Reflection Questions for Emotional Processing Letters

- What is the root cause of these emotions—are they connected to something in the present or the past?
- How have you responded to similar emotions in the past, and how do you wish you could react differently now?
- How does this emotion connect to your values and personal beliefs?
- What is one thing you can do today to begin the process of healing from these emotions?
- Is there something you need to forgive yourself for about this emotional experience?

Self-Reflection Letters

Self-reflection letters are therapeutic letters that help people gain insight into their thoughts, feelings, and behaviors. The individual typically writes these letters to themselves as a means of self-exploration and self-discovery.

The purpose of self-reflection letters is to provide individuals with a safe and structured way to explore their inner world. Individuals can better understand themselves and their experiences by writing about their thoughts and feelings. The act of writing helps to organize and clarify ideas and facilitates problem-solving and decision-making. Self-reflection letters can cover many topics, such as personal values, relationships, goals, fears, and challenges. The notes may include questions to guide the writing process or be more freeing.

After writing the letter, individuals may keep it for reflection or share it with a therapist or trusted friend. The letter can provide a starting point for further discussion and exploration and help individuals identify patterns and themes in their thoughts and behaviors.

Self-reflection letters can be a powerful tool for self-exploration and personal growth. By reflecting on their thoughts and feelings, individuals can gain greater self-awareness and develop more meaningful and fulfilling lives.

Here is an example of a Self-Reflection Letter:

Dear [Your Name],

I have been feeling a lot of stress and anxiety lately, and I realized that I had not taken the time to reflect on what has been going on in my life. I wanted to write to myself and sort through some of my thoughts and feelings.

First, I want to acknowledge that I have been feeling overwhelmed and burnt out. I have been working long hours, taking on too much responsibility, and neglecting my needs.

Secondly, I want to remind myself of my goals and priorities. I have been so focused on work and other obligations that I have lost sight of what matters. I want to be available for the people and activities that bring me joy and fulfillment and not just focus on achieving success in my career.

Finally, I want to express gratitude for all that I have in my life. I am lucky to have a supportive family, a loving partner, and good friends. My job pays the bills and allows me to pursue my passions. I have my health and my creativity. I am grateful for all these blessings and want to ensure I do not take them for granted. I want to commit to taking better care of myself, focusing on my priorities, and expressing gratitude for all I have. Writing this letter has helped me gain clarity and perspective. I will return to it when I need a reminder of what is essential.

Sincerely, [Your Name]

Tips For Getting the Most Out of This

- **Set aside dedicated time:** Choose a time and place to sit and write without distractions. This could be in the morning before your day starts or in the evening before bed.
- **Write without judgment:** When writing a self-reflection letter, it is essential to let your thoughts and emotions flow without judgment. Do not worry about spelling, grammar, or structure - report from the heart.
- **Be honest and open:** Self-reflection letters are a chance to express your thoughts and feelings. Do not shy away from difficult emotions or experiences.
- **Reflect on your progress:** As you write self-reflection letters over time, reflecting on your progress is essential. Look back at previous letters and see how far you have come.
- **Use prompts:** If you need help figuring out where to start, consider using prompts to guide your writing. Many self-reflection prompts are available online, or you can develop your own.
- **Practice self-compassion:** Remember that self-reflection is about gaining insight and understanding, not criticizing or judging yourself. Practice self-compassion and be kind to yourself throughout the process.

Writing Prompts for Self-Reflection Letters:

- **To My Future Self**: Write a letter to yourself five years from now. What advice would you give your future self? What hopes do you have for your growth and well-being?
- **To My Younger Self**: Imagine you could speak to the person you were at a pivotal moment in your life. What words of wisdom or comfort would you offer? How would you reassure them about the challenges ahead?
- **To My Inner Strength**: Write a letter to the part of you that has persevered through hardships. Acknowledge the strength and resilience that have carried you through challenging times.

- **To the Person I am Becoming**: Write about who you are becoming and how you envision your future. What qualities are you nurturing within yourself? What challenges are you embracing?
- **To My Fear or Self-Doubt**: Write a letter to your fear or self-doubt. Acknowledge its presence and express your intention to move forward despite it. How can you transform this fear into something constructive?
- **To My Healing Journey**: Reflect on your healing process, acknowledging where you have been and where you are now. What steps have you taken toward healing, and what does healing look like to you now?
- **To My Self-Worth**: Write a letter to remind yourself of your inherent value. What qualities do you admire in yourself? How can you honor your worth in your daily life?

Self-Reflection Questions:

- What are my most significant lessons in the past year, and how have they shaped who I am today?
- In what areas of my life do I feel most confident, and where do I wish to see growth?
- What do I value most about myself, and how can I nurture these qualities more?
- When I look at my life, what patterns or themes do I see repeating? How can I use this awareness to make intentional changes?
- How do I typically react to challenges, and what would I like to change about my reactions moving forward?
- What is something I have been avoiding, and why? What would happen if I confronted it directly?
- How do I talk to myself when making mistakes, and how can I practice self-compassion in these moments?
- What is proper self-care, and how can I prioritize it more?
- What do I need to forgive myself, and how can I begin letting go?

- If I could give my younger self one piece of advice, what would it be, and how does that advice resonate with my life today?

Relationship Building Letters

Relationship-building letters are letters that are written to improve or strengthen a relationship. These letters can be written to partners, family members, friends, colleagues, or anyone with whom you have a relationship that you want to improve.

Relationship-building letters can take many forms, but some common themes include expressing gratitude, acknowledging and apologizing for past mistakes or misunderstandings, and sharing thoughts and feelings that may be difficult to convey in person.

These letters create a deeper level of intimacy and understanding between two people. By reflecting on your relationship and expressing your thoughts and feelings in a letter, you can communicate more effectively and resolve conflicts more easily. Overall, relationship-building letters can be a powerful tool for improving communication, fostering trust, and strengthening bonds between people.

Here is an example of a relationship-building letter:

Dear [Name],

I wanted to write you this letter to express how much you mean to me and thank you for everything you do. You have been such a wonderful friend to me, and I am grateful for the time we have spent together and the memories we have made.

Sometimes, I can be hard to read, and I might not always express my feelings or thoughts best. But I want you to know that I value your friendship more than anything and appreciate your patience and understanding.

I also want to apologize for any misunderstandings or hurt feelings that may have occurred between us. I may not have always been the best listener and have said or done hurtful or insensitive things. I am genuinely sorry for any pain I may have caused. I hope we move past these things and continue building a solid and healthy relationship.

I am committed to being more open and communicative with you as we progress. I want to ensure we are always on the same page and supporting each other through life's difficulties. I am excited to see where our friendship goes from here, and I know we can accomplish anything together. Thank you again for being such a fantastic friend. I look forward to our next adventure together.

With love and gratitude,

[Your Name]

Tips For Getting the Most Out of This

- **Be specific**: When writing a relationship-building letter, be clear about what you appreciate about the person, what you are apologizing for, or what you want to improve in the relationship. The more specific you can be, the more meaningful your letter will be to the recipient.
- **Use "I" statements**: Focus on your feelings and experiences rather than making assumptions or judgments about the other person. For example, say, "I feel hurt when..." instead of "You always make me feel hurt."
- **Be sincere**: Write honestly about your thoughts and feelings. Avoid insincere flattery or fake apologies, as they can undermine the trust and authenticity of the relationship.
- **Do not expect a specific response**: Remember that you are writing the letter to express your thoughts and feelings, not to control or manipulate the other person's reaction. While you may hope for a positive response, be prepared to accept whatever answer you receive.
- **Consider the timing**: Choose when the other person is receptive to your message. Avoid writing a letter when upset or angry, as it may appear accusatory or aggressive.

- **Keep it private**: Relationship-building letters are often best kept confidential between you and the recipient. This allows the recipient to read and process the letter on their terms without feeling pressured to respond immediately or in a certain way.

Overall, relationship-building letters can be a powerful tool for improving communication, fostering trust, and strengthening bonds between people. By following these tips, you can maximize the impact of your letter and create a more meaningful connection with the other person.

Writing Prompts for Relationship-Building Letters:

- **To a Current Relationship**: "What do I appreciate most about our relationship? How has it shaped me?" "How do I feel when we communicate openly and honestly? "What does that do for our connection?" "What are some specific moments we've shared that have made me feel close to this person?" "Are there any unresolved feelings or issues between us that I want to express and understand better?"
- **To a Past Relationship**: "What lessons have I learned from this relationship, and how have they helped me grow?" "If we could have communicated better, what would I have said differently?" "What role did this person play in my life, and how did they shape who I am today?" "What part of this relationship do I miss, and what part do I not miss?"
- **To a Family Member**: "What do I feel most grateful for about this person, even if we've struggled?" "What can I do to strengthen our bond or understanding?" "How can I show more love and support in this relationship?" "How do I want this relationship to evolve, and what steps can I take to move us in that direction?"
- **To a Friend:** "What do I value most about our friendship?" "How has this friendship been a source of support for me?" "What could I do to be a better friend, and how can I communicate this to them?"

"What does friendship mean to me, and how does this relationship fulfill that meaning?"

- **To a Partner (Romantic Relationship):** "What first attracted me to my partner, and how has that evolved?" "What qualities do I admire most in my partner, and how do they make me a better person?" "How can we continue to strengthen our bond and ensure that both of us feel heard and understood?" "What does love look like in our relationship, and how can we nurture it together?"

Self-Reflection Questions for Relationship-Building Letters:

- **Personal Reflection:** "What role do I play in the most important relationships? Am I giving and receiving equally?" "How do I show up in my relationships, and what would I like to change about how I engage with others?"
- **Communication and Connection:** "What are my strengths and challenges when communicating with others?" "How do I manage misunderstandings, and what could I do to improve my approach?"
- **Forgiveness and Healing:** "Is there any past hurt I am holding onto in my relationships that I need to forgive—either myself or the other person?" "How do I feel about setting boundaries in my relationships, and how can I communicate them in a healthy way?" "What past mistakes or regrets must I release to advance my relationships?"

Goal Setting and Action Planning Letters

Goal-setting letters are therapeutic letters that involve writing about your goals and aspirations for the future. These letters can be a powerful tool for motivation, self-reflection, and personal growth.

In a goal-setting letter, you may explore your short-term and long-term goals, hopes, and dreams and the steps you plan to take to achieve them. You may also reflect on past accomplishments and challenges and use this reflection to guide your future actions.

Goal-setting letters can benefit people feeling stuck or uncertain about their direction in life or struggling to progress toward their goals. By putting your goals into writing, you can clarify your vision, stay focused on your priorities, and hold yourself accountable for making progress.

In addition to helping with personal growth and motivation, goal-setting letters can be a valuable tool for therapy and coaching. Therapists and coaches may use goal-setting letters to help clients identify their values, clarify their priorities, and set achievable goals that align with their vision for the future.

Overall, goal-setting letters can be a powerful tool for personal growth, motivation, and self-reflection. Whether using them for personal development or as part of a therapeutic or coaching process, they can help you stay focused, accountable, and inspired as you work towards your goals.

Here is an example of a Goal Setting and Action-Planning Letter:

Dear [Myself],

I am writing this letter to reflect on my goals and aspirations for the future. As I think about what I want to achieve, I am reminded of the importance of setting clear goals and taking intentional action to make them a reality.

Looking ahead, I have a few key goals that I am enthusiastic about achieving. My first goal is to focus on my physical health and well-being. This means prioritizing regular exercise, healthy eating, and getting enough rest. Taking care of my physical fitness will benefit my body and my mental and emotional well-being.

My second goal is to advance in my career. I want to continue developing my skills and knowledge in my field and take on new challenges and responsibilities. This means proactively seeking professional development opportunities, networking with colleagues, and staying current on industry trends.

My third goal is to deepen my relationships with the people I care about. This means investing more time and energy into building and maintaining strong connections with my family, friends, and community. I know these relationships are essential to my happiness and well-being, and I want to prioritize them accordingly.

Reflecting on these goals, I am reminded of the importance of staying focused and taking intentional action. I know that achieving these goals will require hard work, dedication, and perseverance. Still, I am committed to making them a reality.

- To that end, I plan to take the following steps over the coming weeks and months:
- Schedule regular exercise and prioritize healthy eating and sleep habits.
- Research and enroll in professional development courses or workshops.
- Schedule regular check-ins with family and friends and plan intentional time for socializing and building connections.

I know achieving these goals will be challenging, but I am confident in making them happen. By staying focused, accountable, and taking intentional action, I can create the life I want and achieve my goals.

Sincerely,

[Your Name]

Tips For Getting the Most Out of This

- **Be specific**: When writing your goal-setting letter, be as detailed as possible about what you want to achieve. This will help you stay focused and make a concrete plan for reaching your goals.
- **Use positive language**: Write your goal-setting letter using positive language and focus on what you want to achieve rather than what you want to avoid. This can help

you stay motivated and inspired as you work toward your goals.

- **Be realistic**: Setting challenging, practical, achievable goals is essential. Consider your current circumstances, resources, and timeline when setting your goals, and be prepared to adjust your plan if needed.
- **Create an action plan**: The best way to achieve your goals is to create a clear action plan that outlines the steps you need to take to make them a reality. Break your goals down into smaller, manageable tasks, and create a timeline for when you will complete each one.
- **Stay accountable**: Share your goals and action plan with someone else, such as a friend or therapist, who can help keep you accountable and provide support and encouragement.
- **Reflect on your progress**: Regularly reflect on your progress toward your goals and adjust your action plan as needed. Celebrate your successes and use setbacks or challenges as opportunities to gain experience and grow.

Writing Prompts for Goal-Setting Letters:

- What is the most important goal I want to achieve right now?
- Why is this goal important to me? How will it impact my life?
- What are the specific steps I need to take to accomplish this goal?
- What obstacles might I face while working toward this goal, and how can I overcome them?
- How will I measure my progress toward this goal?
- What resources or support do I need to reach this goal?
- How can I break this goal into more minor, manageable actions?
- When do I want to have accomplished this goal? What is my timeline?
- What strengths do I have that will help me succeed in reaching this goal?

- What would I do if fear or self-doubt prevented me from taking action?

Writing Prompts for Action Planning Letters:

- What is the first step to reach my goal today?

- What small daily or weekly actions can I commit to that will move me forward?
- How can I stay motivated while working toward my goal?
- How can I celebrate milestones or achievements along the way?
- What do I need to let go of or change to move forward with my goal?
- Who can I contact for accountability or encouragement as I work toward this goal?
- How will I manage setbacks or unexpected challenges?
- How will I stay focused on my goal when distractions arise?
- How do I envision my life after achieving this goal? What will be different?
- What is one thing I can do each day to stay aligned with my long-term vision?

Self-Reflection Questions for Reflection After Setting Goals:

- What excites me most about achieving this goal?
- What fears or doubts do I have about reaching this goal, and how can I address them?
- What personal growth do I hope to experience in achieving this goal?
- What positive habits or routines will I need to develop to stay on track?
- How does this goal align with my core values or life purpose?
- How will achieving this goal improve my sense of self-worth or confidence?

- What will be the long-term benefits of accomplishing this goal?
- If I achieve this goal, how will it influence other areas of my life?
- What inner resources must I tap into to stay focused and committed?
- What is one act of self-compassion I can practice if I face difficulties on my way to achieving this goal?

Creative and Expressive Letters

Creative and expressive letters use art, poetry, storytelling, or other innovative means to explore and express emotions, thoughts, and experiences. These letters can be a powerful self-expression, healing, and personal growth tool.

Creative and expressive letters can take many forms, depending on the individual's preferences and creative abilities. Some examples of innovative and expressive letters include:

- Drawing or painting a picture representing your emotions or experiences and writing a letter to yourself or someone else that describes what the picture means to you.
- Write a poem that explores a particular emotion or experience and use the letter to reflect on the poem and its significance.
- Tell a story about a particular experience and use the letter to reflect on it and how it has impacted you.
- Create a collage, painting, poem, or other mixed media art piece representing your emotions or experiences, and use the letter to describe the art and what it means to you.

Creative and expressive letters can tap into your inner creativity and be used for self-exploration and healing. These letters can benefit people who struggle to express themselves verbally or who find traditional therapy methods limiting.

Here is an example of a creative and expressive letter:

Dear [Your Name],

Today, I woke up feeling heavy and weighed down. I could not understand why, but I knew something was off. Instead of trying to push the feeling aside or distract me from it, I decided to sit down and create something that would help me explore it.

I started by gathering some materials - a blank canvas, acrylic paints, and brushes. I did not have a clear plan, but I knew I wanted to let my emotions guide me. I closed my eyes, took a few deep breaths, and started to paint.

As I worked, I felt the heaviness in my chest lifting. The colors and shapes on the canvas did not make logical sense, but they were true to what I felt inside. I used bold strokes and vibrant colors, letting my emotions spill onto the canvas without judgment or inhibition.

When I finished, I looked back at what I had created. It was not a masterpiece but a true expression of what was happening inside me. I saw layers of sadness, anger, and confusion but also hints of hope and resilience.

As I sat with the painting, I started to write. I wrote about what each color and shape represented. I explored what the painting told me about my emotions and experiences. I wrote about the things weighing me down and acknowledged the pain and hurt I had been carrying. By the time I was finished, I felt a sense of release and clarity. I had taken a step towards understanding and healing, and I had done it in a way that felt authentic to myself.

Love, Me

Tips For Getting the Most Out of This

- **Permit yourself to be messy**: When creating something expressive and artistic, letting go of the need for perfection is essential. Do not worry about whether your painting or drawing looks "good" - focus on letting your emotions guide your creative process. Allow yourself to make mistakes, experiment with different materials, and let your creativity flow freely.

- **Use your senses**: Incorporate different senses into your creative process to make it more immersive and engaging. For example, you might listen to music that reflects your emotions, light a candle with a soothing scent, or use materials with interesting textures.

- **Let go of self-judgment**: It is easy to get caught up in unfavorable self-talk when creating something vulnerable and personal. Remind yourself that the point of this exercise is not to create something that is "good" or "perfect" - it is to express your emotions and connect with yourself meaningfully. Let go of any self-judgment or criticism and embrace the process for what it is.

- **Reflect on your creation**: Once you have finished your creative expression, take some time to reflect on what you have created. Write about what the colors, shapes, and textures mean and how they relate to your emotions and experiences. Allow yourself to explore the themes and ideas that emerge from your creation and use your writing to delve deeper into your thoughts and feelings.

- **Repeat as necessary**: Creative and expressive letters can be a powerful tool for self-reflection and emotional processing, but they are not a one-time fix. Make it a habit to incorporate creative expression into your self-care routine and use it to connect with yourself and process your emotions continuously.

Writing Prompts for Creative and Expressive Letters:

- Write a letter to your heart, imagining it as a separate entity. What does it want to say about how it has been feeling lately?

- Imagine your grief or pain as a character in a story. Write a letter from that character, explaining why it exists and what it wants from you.

- Write a letter to a "dream version" of yourself. What advice would this version of you give to the person you are now? What would they want you to know about the future?

- If your emotions were colors, textures, or shapes, what would they look like? Write a letter to yourself describing the landscape of your emotions as if they were physical entities.
- Write a letter to your childhood self. What creative stories, memories, or metaphors would you share about the person you have become today?
- Write a letter to the sky (or another element of nature) to express your emotions. Use metaphors to describe how you feel, as if you were telling the weather or the landscape.
- Write a letter to an object that holds deep meaning for you (a piece of jewelry, a childhood toy, or a family heirloom). What story does it tell about your life and experiences?
- Imagine your grief in a garden. Write a letter to the plants, flowers, or trees in the garden, describing the emotions they represent and what you want to learn from them.
- Write a letter to your fear, giving it a voice. Ask it questions, acknowledge its presence, and see what it needs to say to you.
- Write a letter as if you were a poet, using metaphors to describe the most powerful emotions you are experiencing. Create vivid imagery to communicate your feelings to yourself.

Self-Reflection Questions for Creative and Expressive Letters:

- What part of myself do I often ignore or hide from others? What would that part want me to know if it could speak openly through a letter?
- How would it appear if I could personify my grief, and what message would it have for me?
- How can I express my emotions creatively—without judgment or expectation—through storytelling, metaphors, or images?

- What do I wish I could say to myself that I have never given voice to? How can I use creativity to unlock those hidden feelings?
- What would it look like if I could create a symbolic representation of my journey through grief or loss? How can I describe it in a letter to myself?
- What emotions do I often try to suppress or avoid? How might they be communicated creatively in a letter to help me understand them better?
- How would my emotions change if I could step outside and view them as an observer or storyteller? What does that shift in perspective reveal?
- How can I express my healing process through art, imagination, or metaphors? What letter would I write to reflect that transformation?
- What feelings have I been carrying that I have not had the chance to process yet? What would happen if I allowed these feelings to be expressed through creative writing?
- If I could write a letter to my future self, how would I describe the emotional journey I am going through in an artistic, metaphorical way?

Trauma Letters

A trauma letter is a therapeutic letter specifically focused on processing traumatic experiences. Trauma letters can be a powerful tool for individuals who have experienced trauma and are struggling to cope with the aftereffects.

In a trauma letter, the individual is encouraged to write about their experience in a structured and intentional way. This may include describing the traumatic event and the emotional and physical responses they experienced. The letter may also explore how the trauma has impacted their life since then, including any ongoing symptoms such as flashbacks, nightmares, or anxiety.

The goal of a trauma letter is to help the individual process their experience in a safe and supportive way. By putting their thoughts and emotions into words, they may gain greater clarity and understanding of what happened and how it has affected them. Writing can also be cathartic and healing, allowing the individual to release pent-up emotions and find relief and closure.

It is important to note that trauma letters should be done in a safe and supportive environment and may be best done under the guidance of a trained mental health professional. Collaborating with a therapist or counselor can help ensure that the process is managed appropriately and that the individual has access to the support they need to process their trauma healthily and effectively.

Here is an example of a trauma letter:

I did not include any examples of trauma letters here. Trauma letters are overly sensitive and emotionally charged letters. Including one here might be triggering. I often recommend doing a trauma letter with a therapist, guided in therapy, as emotional dysregulation can be severe. If you must write a letter of this nature, ensure you have family or another trusted support system that can be sought if overwhelming emotions arise.

Tips For Getting the Most Out of This

- **Work with a trained mental health professional:** Writing trauma letters can be a challenging and emotionally intense process. Having the support and guidance of a qualified mental health professional who can help you navigate the procedure safely and effectively is essential.
- **Set a clear intention**: Before you begin writing, set a clear intention for what you hope to accomplish through the process. This might involve identifying specific aspects of the trauma you want to process or setting goals for how you want to feel after completing the process.
- **Create a safe and supportive environment**: Writing about traumatic experiences can be triggering, so creating a safe and supportive environment before you begin is essential. This might involve finding a quiet and private space where you feel comfortable or engaging in self-care

practices like deep breathing or mindfulness to help ground you in the present moment.

- **Take breaks when needed**: Writing about trauma can be emotionally taxing, so it is essential to take breaks when needed. If you feel overwhelmed or triggered during the writing process, take a break and engage in self-care practices like walking, listening to calming music, or talking to a trusted friend or therapist.

- **Practice self-compassion**: Writing about trauma can be challenging, and it is important to practice self-compassion throughout the process. This might involve acknowledging your emotions without judgment or offering yourself words of kindness and support as you work through complicated feelings.

- **Consider sharing your letter with a trusted person:** While trauma letters can be highly personal, some people find it helpful to share their letters with a trusted person, like a therapist, friend, or family member. Sharing your letter can help you feel seen and heard. It may provide an opportunity for more profound healing and connection. However, it is essential to share your letter only if you feel comfortable and safe doing so.

Writing Prompts for Trauma Letters:

- **To the Trauma Itself:** "I never expected to experience this pain, and yet here I am. I want you to know how you've affected me and shaped my life in ways I didn't foresee."

- **To My Younger Self (Before the Trauma):** "Before everything changes, I want you to know I see you. I see your innocence, your strength, and your trust. I wish I could protect you from what's coming, but here's what I want you to remember about yourself, even when things get tough."

- **To the Person or People Involved**: "I still feel the weight of what happened and need to share this with you. I am unsure if you ever understood how much your actions hurt me, but this is how it affected me, and here is how it continues to impact my life.

- **To My Future Self:** "I don't know what the future will bring, but I know I will carry this pain with me in some form. Looking back, I want you to remember that this healing moment was a turning point. Here's what I hope for you in the future."
- **To the Fear or Pain, Itself:** "Fear, you've made a home within me, but I want to understand you better. What do you need from me to finally release your hold on me? What do I need to say to make you let go?"

Self-Reflection Questions for Trauma Letters:

- **Exploring the Impact of the Trauma:** "In what ways has this trauma influenced how I perceive myself? How has it altered my beliefs or sense of identity?"
- **Understanding Emotional Responses:** "What emotions arise when I reflect on the trauma? How have those emotions evolved?"
- **Addressing Unspoken Thoughts**: "Are there things I've never been able to say about this experience? What would it feel like to release those thoughts or words?" "What do I still need to forgive myself for about this trauma? For what do I need to forgive others?"
- **Empowerment and Healing:** "What does healing look like for me? What small steps can I take today to move in that direction?" "How can I reclaim my sense of agency and power? What parts of me still feel empowered, even in the face of trauma?"
- **Looking Toward the Future:** "What lessons, strengths, or insights have I gained from this experience? How can I use them moving forward?"

Deceased Letters

Deceased letters are therapeutic letters written to a person who has passed away. They can be a way for the writer to express feelings of grief, loss, regret, or any other emotions they may have been unable to express while the person was alive. Deceased letters can also be used for healing, closure, and to process emotions related to losing a loved one.

Here is an example of a letter to a deceased loved one:

Dear [Your Name],

It has been a year since you left us, and not a day goes by that I do not miss you. Losing you was the hardest thing I have ever gone through, and I still cannot believe you are gone.

I wish I could have told you how much you meant to me when you were alive. I wish I had spent more time with you, listened more, and appreciated you for all that you did for me. I know I did not always show it, but you were the center of my world, and I will never forget your love and kindness.

I hope you are at peace now and that you can see how much you are loved and missed. I will never forget the memories we shared and will always cherish our time together. Thank you for being the best mom in the world, and I promise to make you proud.

Love always, [Your Name].

Tips For Getting the Most Out of This

- **Write from the heart:** Let your emotions flow, and do not hold back. Be honest about how you feel, even if it is painful.
- **Be specific:** Share specific memories, events, or moments you remember with your loved one. This can help bring back fond memories and create a more profound connection.
- **Acknowledge the loss:** Recognize the pain and sadness you feel from the loss. Accepting these feelings can help you move toward healing.

- **Express gratitude:** Thank your loved one for the time you spent together, the things they taught you, and the love they gave you.
- **Say goodbye:** Use the letter as an opportunity to say goodbye, express any unresolved emotions or issues, and find closure.
- **Keep the letter or find a unique way to honor your loved one:** You can choose to keep the letter for yourself as a personal memento or find a unique way to celebrate your loved one, such as burning or burying the letter.

Writing Prompts for Deceased Letters:

- What is something you have always wanted to say but never had the chance to?
- What moments do you miss the most, and why do they stand out?
- How has your life changed since you have been gone? What do you wish you could see or know about how things are now?
- What do you want me to remember about you? What lessons or wisdom do you hope I carry forward?
- What would you say to me if you were still here? How would I be different if you were still with me?
- Is there anything you left unsaid that I now wish I had heard?
- What are the goodbyes I never had to say to you?
- What do you want me to know about your life, choices, or feelings?
- How can I honor your memory in a way that feels meaningful to me?
- Write about the grief you feel now that they are gone. How do you think the absence of their presence in your life?

Self-Reflection Questions for Deceased Letters:

- What emotions surface when I write this letter? How do I feel about expressing them?
- Do I feel any unresolved anger, regret, or forgiveness that I need to process in this letter?
- What has this person taught me, directly or indirectly, that still shapes my life today?
- What do I wish I could have done or said before they passed, and how does it feel to express these now?
- In what ways has their passing impacted my view of life, love, and relationships?
- Do I feel a sense of closure after writing this letter? Why or why not?
- How do I feel about my relationship with this person now that I am writing to them after their death?
- What, if anything, do I feel at peace after writing this letter?
- Do I feel more connected to them after writing this letter, or has it brought up new feelings that need further reflection?

Spiritual Letters

Spiritual letters are therapeutic letters used to explore spiritual or existential issues, such as meaning, purpose, and connection to something greater than oneself. These letters can be written to oneself, a higher power or spiritual figure, or a trusted friend or therapist.

Spiritual letters provide individuals with a safe and structured way to explore their spiritual or existential beliefs, values, and experiences. These letters can help individuals to connect with their inner selves and to explore their relationship with the universe or a higher power.

Spiritual letters can cover a wide range of topics, such as:

- Seeking guidance or wisdom from a higher power or spiritual figure
- Exploring one's beliefs and values.
- Reflecting on spiritual or existential experiences
- Expressing gratitude or appreciation for the blessings in one's life.
- Seeking forgiveness or reconciliation for past mistakes or transgressions
- Seeking comfort or reassurance during tough times
- Exploring one's purpose or meaning in life.

After writing the letter, individuals may keep it for reflection or share it with a therapist or trusted friend. The letter can provide a starting point for further discussion and exploration. It can help individuals to find meaning and purpose in their lives.

Overall, spiritual letters can be a powerful tool for self-exploration and personal growth. They help individuals connect with their inner selves and something greater than themselves.

Here is an example of a spiritual letter:

"Dear [God, Universe, Higher Power], I approach you today with a heart brimming with [emotion]. I seek your guidance regarding [specific situation]. Please assist me in finding clarity and peace during this time."

Tips For Getting the Most Out of This

- **Set aside dedicated time**: Schedule a specific time and place to write your spiritual letter. This can help you to focus and create a calm and contemplative space for your writing.
- **Connect with your intentions**: Before you start writing, take a few moments to connect with your intentions. Consider why you want to write this letter and what you hope to gain from the process.
- **Write freely and authentically**: Allow yourself to write freely and without judgment. Do not worry about

grammar, spelling, or punctuation. Instead, focus on expressing yourself authentically and from the heart.

- Be open to insights and guidance: As you write, stay open to any insights or advice that may come to you. You may find that your writing takes unexpected turns, or you receive insights you were not expecting.
- Reflect on your writing: After you have finished writing, take some time to reflect on what you have written. Consider the themes and messages in your writing and how they relate to your spiritual or existential beliefs and values.
- Share with a trusted individual: You may share your spiritual letter with a trusted individual, such as a therapist, spiritual mentor, or trusted friend. Sharing your writing can help to deepen your understanding and provide an opportunity for feedback and support.
- Practice gratitude: Before you end your writing session, take a moment to express gratitude for the opportunity to write and for any insights or guidance that you may have received. This can help to cultivate a sense of inner peace and connection to something greater than yourself.

Writing spiritual letters can be a powerful tool for self-exploration and personal growth. Connecting with your spiritual beliefs and values can cultivate a greater sense of purpose, meaning, and connection.

Writing Prompts for Spiritual Letters:

- **Letter of Gratitude for Spiritual Gifts**: "Dear [God, Spirit, Universe], I am thankful for the blessings in my life, particularly for [list specific spiritual gifts or experiences]. I appreciate the guidance you've provided me."
- **Letter of Forgiveness and Healing:** "Dear [Higher Power], I am carrying hurt in my heart from [situation or person]. Please help me release the anger and find healing to open my heart to peace and love again."

- **Letter to Your Future Self in Spiritual Growth**: "Dear Future Me, I'm on a path of spiritual growth, and I'd like to know where you are now. What advice would you offer me on this journey to deepen my faith and connection?"
- **Letter Asking for Guidance During a Spiritual Struggle:** "Dear [Higher Power], I am facing [specific challenge or question]. Please help me find the strength to trust in your plan."

Self-Reflection Questions for Spiritual Letters:

- **Connection to Higher Power**: "How do I experience the presence of the Divine or a higher power? What moments or events have made me feel closest to this connection?"
- **Purpose and Meaning:** "What is the deeper purpose I feel called to in this life? How can I align my actions with my spiritual beliefs to live more purposefully?"
- **Faith in Challenging Times:** "How do I maintain faith and trust in a higher power or the universe when faced with challenges or uncertainty? What have been moments when faith helped me through tough times?"
- **Spiritual Healing:** "Are there any areas where I feel spiritually blocked or need healing? How can I invite healing into those parts of my life?"
- **Forgiveness and Making Peace With:** "What unresolved spiritual or emotional wounds do I carry? How can I release these burdens to find peace and forgiveness for myself and others?"
- **Gratitude for Spiritual Guidance**: "What spiritual teachings, experiences, or people have shaped my understanding of the Divine? What am I most grateful for in my spiritual life?"
- **Vision for Spiritual Growth:** "How do I envision my spiritual growth unfolding over the next year? What practices, rituals, or experiences would support this growth?"

Narrative Letters

Narrative letters are a form of storytelling where the writer recounts a particular event, experience, or memory. These letters allow the writer to process their feelings and gain insight from the story they tell. The writer often finds clarity or resolve by putting these events into their own words. Writing a narrative letter can help understand the complexity of emotions tied to a particular event. This offers a structured way to reflect on what has happened and how it has impacted them. These letters are unique because they allow their writer to step back and look at the bigger picture.

Here is an example of a narrative letter:

Dear [Name],

I remember the day we met as if it was yesterday. It was a warm autumn afternoon, and I had just moved into the neighborhood. I felt out of place, uncertain how to settle into a new life. But then, you came over with that friendly smile of yours, introduced yourself, and we began to talk. You told me about the neighborhood, your life, and how you had been through similar changes not long ago. That conversation helped me feel a little less alone, and I knew then that you were someone special.

As time passed, our friendship blossomed. We shared many moments—laughing over coffee, supporting each other through tough times, and celebrating the small victories. I will never forget the way you helped me through that challenging time when I was struggling with a personal loss. Your kindness and generosity were like a guiding light in a dark time. Looking back, I realize how important those moments were and how much you impacted my life. Thank you for being there, showing me true friendship, and bringing so much light into my world.

With love,

[Your Name]

Tips For Getting the Most Out of This

- **Be descriptive** – Describe the event or experience as vividly as possible. Include sensory details to bring it to life.
- **Write honestly** – Do not filter or edit yourself in the first draft. Let the emotions and story unfold naturally.
- **Explore different perspectives** – Consider how you felt then versus now. Has your perspective changed?
- **Focus on meaning** – Find a lesson, realization, or insight in your experience. Authoring the story can help process emotions and bring clarity.
- **Do not worry about structure** – This is your reflection. Write in a way that feels natural.

Writing Prompts for Narrative Letters:

- Write about a moment in your life that changed you. What happened, and how did you grow from it?
- Describe a time when you faced a significant challenge. How did you manage it, and what did you learn?
- Tell the story of a friendship, family, or romantic relationship that shaped who you are today.

Self-Reflection Questions for Narrative Letters:

- What emotions come up when I recall this experience?
- How has my perspective on this event changed over time?
- If I could go back, what would I say to myself during that moment?

Unsent Letters

Unsent letters are powerful tools for emotional release. These letters are typically addressed to someone who cannot or should not receive the letter. These might include a deceased loved one, an estranged friend, or a painful memory. An unsent letter allows the writer to express feelings that might remain unspoken. These letters are cathartic, allowing the writer to pour their heart onto the paper. However, it is essential to note that unsent letters can also stir up intense emotions and may not be suitable for everyone. This letter's beauty is the freedom it gives the writer. They do not need to be edited, validated, or shared, allowing for raw, unfiltered expression of emotion and processing.

Here is an example of an unsent letter:

Dear [Name],

I have spent many months wondering if I would find the words to say to you. Some of me still wants to reach out and reconnect, but another part knows it's too late for that. So, I am writing this unsent letter to express what I have finally held in my heart.

I am hurt by how things ended between us; we drifted apart without any explanation. You were more than a friend to me; you were family. And when you suddenly stopped reaching out, when I could not understand why things changed, I felt abandoned. I spent so much time wondering what I did wrong, questioning myself, and carrying that weight around.

I miss our friendship but must also let go of the pain. I need to stop carrying this sadness. It is hard, but I am learning to accept that people change, and sometimes, they walk out of our lives without ever realizing how much they left behind.

I hope you are doing well wherever you are. And one day, if our paths cross again, we can reflect on what we shared with more understanding and peace.

[Your Name]

Tips For Getting the Most Out of This

- **Let go of judgment** – Write as if you are saying everything you have held back. This letter is for you, not the recipient.
- **Be completely honest** – Express emotions openly, whether anger, sadness, love, or regret.

- **Decide if you want to keep or discard it** – Some people find release in tearing up or burning an unsent letter, while others keep it for reflection.
- **Write without expectation** – You need not worry about a response since this letter will not be sent. Allow yourself to say everything you need.
- **Consider revisiting it later** – Reading your letter after some time can give you insight into your healing process.

Writing Prompts for an Unsent Letter:

- Write a letter to someone who hurt you, expressing everything you never got to say.
- Draft a letter to someone you miss but can no longer speak to.
- Write a letter to someone you never got closure with.

Self-Reflection Questions for Unsent Letters:

- What emotions arise as I write this?
- What would I want from this person if they could read my letter?
- How does writing this letter help me move forward?

Gratitude Letters

Gratitude letters emphasize expressing thanks and acknowledging the positive influence of someone or something in your life. Composing a gratitude letter allows the writer to contemplate the blessings and experiences that have shaped their journey, enhancing feelings of thankfulness and emotional wellness. These letters can be directed to anyone. Studies indicate that writing gratitude letters has multiple benefits, such as heightened happiness and decreased stress. Focusing on what they appreciate allows the writer to alter their viewpoint and nurture positivity. Furthermore, gratitude letters reinforce relationships.

Here is an example of a Gratitude Letter:

Dear [Name],

I have been reflecting on how much you mean to me lately. I am writing to share my gratitude for everything you have done for me. You have consistently been a source of strength and support, and I have never truly conveyed how much that means to me.

During my most challenging moments, you were the one who stepped in without hesitation. Whether it was a quick phone call, grabbing coffee, or having a deep, heartfelt conversation, you were always there. Your kindness and generosity have functioned as a lifeline, and I feel incredibly fortunate to have you in my life. Thank you for all the ways you've supported our friendship—it has been one of the greatest gifts I could ever ask for.

Thanks,

[Your Name]

Tips For Getting the Most Out of This

- **Be specific** – Instead of general gratitude, mention exact moments, qualities, or actions that meant a lot to you.
- **Make it heartfelt** – Do not just list things you appreciate—describe why they are meaningful.
- **Consider sharing it** – Gratitude letters can be powerful, unlike other therapeutic letters. They can strengthen relationships and bring the writer and recipient joy.
- **Reflect on the impact** – Writing about gratitude can improve your mood and outlook, so take time to feel the appreciation as you write.
- **Make it a habit** – Regularly writing gratitude letters can increase positivity and mindfulness, even if they are short.

Writing Prompts for Gratitude Letters:

- Write a letter to someone who has made a lasting impact on your life.
- Express appreciation to someone for a small act of kindness that meant a lot to you.
- Write a letter to yourself, thanking yourself for your resilience and strength.

Self-Reflection Questions for Gratitude Letters:

- How does expressing gratitude make me feel at this moment?
- What have I never thanked this person for but want to acknowledge now?
- How has this person's presence in my life influenced who I am?

Forgiveness Letters

Forgiveness letters release resentment, anger, and hurt towards others. In these letters, the writer acknowledges the pain caused by themselves or others. Writing a forgiveness letter is not about forgetting the situation or excusing the harmful behavior but about freeing oneself from the emotional burden of grudges or past wrongs. It is a practice of *"making peace with"* to create emotional space for healing. You are not required to *"let it go,"* but you can *"make peace with it"* instead.

These letters are essential to emotional self-care, as they help the writer reclaim their inner peace and move forward. Writing a letter of forgiveness can bring relief, especially when the writer has been holding onto the pain for a while.

Here is an example of a forgiveness letter:

Dear [Name],

I have been holding onto anger for a long time, and I can no longer carry this weight. I am writing this letter to forgive you—for the hurtful things you said and did that caused so much pain. For so long, I kept replaying those moments, holding onto resentment, convinced I could never let go. But as time passed, I realized that my anger only hurt me. It is time to release it.

I forgive you. I know what happened between us was complicated, and I do not expect you to understand everything I felt. But I am choosing to let go of the anger and pain. It is no longer serving me. I am ready to move forward and hope you find peace, too.

[Your Name]

Tips For Getting the Most Out of This

- **Acknowledge your feelings first** – Allow yourself to express anger, hurt, or disappointment before offering forgiveness.
- **Remember that forgiveness is for you** – It does not mean excusing unruly behavior or reconciling with the person; it is about freeing yourself from resentment.
- **Even if you are not ready to forgive** – You do not have to force forgiveness. Sometimes, writing about the pain is the first step toward healing.
- **Try different approaches** – If forgiving someone else is difficult, start with forgiving yourself or writing about what forgiveness might feel like.
- **End with a sense of closure** – Whether you say, "I forgive you" or "I release this pain," try to close the letter with a sense of moving forward.

Writing Prompts for Forgiveness Letters:

- Write a letter to someone who hurt you, acknowledging your pain and the process of letting go.
- Write a letter to yourself, forgiving yourself for a mistake or past decision.
- Imagine writing a letter to someone who has passed, releasing unresolved resentment.

Self-Reflection Questions for Forgiveness Letters:

- Am I ready to forgive, or am I still working through my emotions?
- How is holding onto resentment affecting me?
- What would forgiveness look and feel like for me?

Younger/Future Self Letters

Writing a letter to one's younger self involves reflecting on the lessons learned over time. This can offer comfort, guidance, or reassurance to the past version of yourself. These letters are deeply compassionate, as the writer often writes to provide kindness to the self.

Letters to one's future self and take on more of a forward-looking approach. In these letters, the writer envisions where they hope to one day be. This can offer encouragement and motivation to their future self. This form of letter writing can provide a sense of direction, reminding the writer of their dreams and a personal road map.

Here is an example of a younger self-letter:

Dear Younger Me,

I know you are struggling right now. You are facing overwhelming challenges, and it seems like the world is too big and complicated. But I want to tell you this—you are stronger than you realize. The pain you feel now will not last forever, and you will emerge from these struggles with more wisdom and resilience than you ever thought possible. You have the power to heal, to grow, and to overcome.

I want you to remember that you are worthy of love and happiness no matter how hard things get. You do not need to be perfect to be enough. So, take a deep breath, trust yourself, and know that everything you are experiencing shapes you into the person you are meant to be. You are not alone. You have what it takes to get through this.

With love and strength,

[Your Name]

Tips For Getting the Most Out of This

- **Be compassionate** – Talk to your younger or future self as kindly as you would to a friend.
- **Acknowledge challenges and strengths** – If writing to your younger self, validate your struggles and recognize the strengths that carried you through.
- **Set intentions for your future self** – If writing to the future, include encouragement, advice, and reminders of what matters most to you now.
- **Make it personal** – Include inside jokes, memories, or details that make the letter more meaningful when revisited.
- **Save and revisit** – Letters to yourself can be incredibly insightful when read years later. Please keep them in a safe place and check in with them from time to time.

Writing Prompts for Younger/Future Self Letters:

- Write a letter to your younger self at a grim time, offering encouragement and wisdom.
- Write to your future self about your hopes, fears, and dreams.
- Imagine receiving a letter from your future self; what advice or reassurance would you want to hear?

Self-Reflection Questions for Younger/Future Self Letters:

- What would I tell my younger self to help them through tough times?
- What do I hope my future self remembers about this moment in my life?
- How can I show myself more compassion now and in the future?

Throughout my life, I have had several instances where this has personally helped me. I find writing to be one of the most powerful therapeutic tools. Hurt and pain are further chances for us to learn and grow as individuals. Though it might not feel like that now, it indeed can be.

In conclusion, therapeutic letter writing can be a powerful tool for promoting personal growth and healing. By engaging in self-reflection, emotional processing, and spiritual exploration through the written word, individuals can better understand themselves, their experiences, and their place in the world.

Through writing and reflecting on their emotions and experiences, individuals can learn to regulate their emotions more effectively, cultivate greater self-awareness and self-compassion, and develop a more profound sense of purpose and meaning. Whether used in conjunction with therapy or as a standalone practice, therapeutic letter writing can provide a valuable tool for those seeking to navigate life's challenges and promote personal growth.

However, it is essential to remember that therapeutic letter writing is just one tool in the more extensive process of self-exploration and healing. It is important to seek additional resources and support, such as therapy, counseling, or support groups, to ensure you receive the best care for your mental and emotional well-being.

In the end, therapeutic letter writing is a practice that requires patience, self-compassion, and an open mind. By approaching this process with curiosity and a willingness to explore your inner landscape, you can unlock new insights and deeper levels of understanding to help you live a more meaningful and fulfilling life.

I wish you all the best as you continue emotional healing and reflection through this. I hope that you can find as much hope, faith, and relief as I have been able to.

About The Author

C. Hennis is a therapist, author, and widowed mother who truly grasps the profound and life-altering effects of loss. Following her husband's death, grief transformed every part of her life—emotionally, physically, and in her self-perception. During this journey, writing emerged as a crucial outlet, enabling her to process her pain, gain insights, and start healing.

Her second book, *Breaking: Understanding the Loss of a Partner*, presents a heartfelt examination of the unique challenges faced after losing a spouse. It delves into the emotional and physical consequences of grief, the changes in identity, and the intricate process of rebuilding life after such a significant loss. By drawing on her own experiences and her expertise as a therapist, she extends support to those in mourning and those seeking to assist them.

Beyond her professional commitments, C. Hennis values simplicity, connection, and the significance found in daily moments. Through her writing and career, she aspires to comfort those navigating their grief, reassuring them that healing is possible, even when it feels far out of reach.

Works Cited

Baikie, K. A. (2005). Emotional and Physical Health Benefits of Expressive Writing. *Advances in Psychiatric Treatment*. Retrieved from https://www.cambridge.org/core/journals/advances-in-psychiatric-treatment/article/emotional-and-physical-health-benefits-of-expressive-writing/ED2976A61F5DE56B46F07A1CE9EA9F9F

Koschwanez, H. E. (2013). Expressive writing and wound healing in older adults: A randomized controlled trial. *Psychosomatic Medicine*, 75(6), 581-590.

Koṭlawī, A. Y. (n.d.). *Akhlāq-uṣ-Ṣāliḥīn*. Karachi, Pakistan: Maktaba-tul-Madīnah.

Pennebaker, J. W. (1986). Confronting a traumatic event: Toward an understanding of inhibition and disease. *Journal of Abnormal Psychology*, 95(3), 274-281.

Pennebaker, J. W. (1997). *Opening up: The healing power of expressing emotions*. Guilford Press.

Smyth, J. M. (1998). Written emotional expression: Effect sizes, outcome types, and moderating variables. *Journal of Consulting and Clinical Psychology*, 66(1), 174-184.